METERS	YARDS	INCHES
1	1.093	39.37
.914	1	36

CENTIMETERS	INCHES	FEET
1	.394	.033
2.54	1	.083
30.48	12	1

KILOMETERS	MILES
1	.621
1.609	1

GRAMS	OUNCES	POUNDS
1	.035	.002
28.35	1	.062
453.59	16	1
1,000	35.274	2.205

LITERS	PINTS	QUARTS	GALLONS
1	2.113	1.057	.264
.473	1	½	⅛
.946	2	1	¼
3.785	8	4	1

The METRIC System

by David A. Adler • illustrated by Edward Miller

HOLIDAY HOUSE • NEW YORK

Here are Jennifer and Robert.

That's what their parents named them. That's what their teachers call them. But to their friends, they're Jenny and Bob.

Of course, whether you call them Jennifer and Robert or Jenny and Bob, they are the same two people.

It's the same with measurements.

In the United States we would say Jenny is about 4 feet tall. In most other countries, places where the Metric System is used, people would say Jenny is about 1.22 meters tall. So 4 feet and 1.22 meters are just different ways of saying the same thing.

In the United States we would say Bob weighs about 0 pounds. In places that use e Metric System, people ould say Bob weighs about 6 kilograms. So 80 pounds nd a little over 36 kilograms e just different ways of aying the same thing.

Linear Measure— Length and Distance

In the United States when we measure we mostly use the English System. We measure **length** in **inches (in)**, **feet (ft)**, and **yards (yd)**. We measure great **distances** in **miles (mi)**.

At first the foot measure was based on the length of a man's foot. It was divided into 12 inches. The yard was based on the length of the king's arm. The mile, on the distance traveled in one thousand steps.

5,280 feet = 1,760 yards = 1 mile

3 feet =
1 yard

12 inches =
1 foot

Basing a measure on the length of a man's foot can be a problem. Visit any shoe store and you'll find that shoes come in many sizes. People's feet are not all the same length. The same goes for people's arms. The length of our steps are different, too.

In 1824 the British Weights and Measures Act set a standard for the length of a foot, a yard, and a mile.

Hear ye, hear ye! By order of the King.

British Weights & Measures Act

ONE YARD

TWO FEET

ONE FOOT

In the 1790s French scientists introduced what was meant to be an easier system of measurement, the **Metric System**. Its units of length are all based on the **meter** and the power of ten. The Metric System was soon used throughout Europe and among scientists everywhere.

The Metric System

The power of 10!

Meter

$$10$$
$$\times \, 10$$
$$= 100$$

$$10 \times 10 \times 10 = 1{,}000$$

In the Metric System all measures of length are based on the **meter**. Its three most used measures are the **centimeter (cm)**, the **meter (m)**, and the **kilometer (km)**.

Each centimeter is 1/100 of a meter. Each kilometer is 1,000 meters.

With the English System you would use inches to measure this page. It's 10 inches tall and 8 inches wide. With the Metric System you would use centimeters. It's 25.4 centimeters tall and 20.32 centimeters wide.

It's easy to convert inches to centimeters and centimeters to inches.

Many rulers, perhaps one of yours, measure inches on one side and centimeters on the other.

I centimeter

A penny is almost 2 centimeters wide.

It takes about 12 minutes to walk this far.

I kilometer (1,000 meters)

If you don't have such a ruler, you can make one. With a copy machine, make a copy of the ruler on the flap of this book. Use safety scissors and adult supervision to cut out the picture, and you'll have a paper ruler with inches on one side and centimeters on the other.

With your ruler, measure items in inches and in centimeters. Measure the length of a pencil, the sides of a cereal box, the height of a water bottle. Compare the measurements. The pencil may be 6 inches in the English System and slightly more than 15 centimeters in the Metric System. Of course, whether you measure the pencil in inches or centimeters, it's the same length: 6 inches and slightly more than 15 centimeters are just different ways of saying the same thing.

Measure these items in inches and centimeters.
Check your answers on page 31.

With the English System you would use feet to measure the dimensions of an Olympic-size swimming pool. It's about 164 feet long and 82 feet wide. With the Metric System you would measure it in meters. It's 50 meters long and 25 meters wide.

It's easy to convert feet to meters and meters to feet.

82 ft (25 m)

1 foot = 30.48 centimeters or about .30 meters

1 meter = 3.28 feet

164 ft (50 m)

Look at the height of some famous landmarks. The Statue of Liberty is 305 feet tall. That would be 93 meters. The Eiffel Tower is 1,063 feet tall. That would be 324 meters.

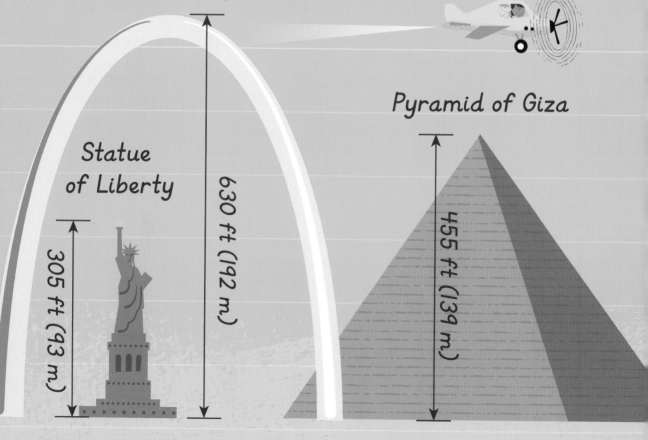

St. Louis Gateway Arch

Statue of Liberty

630 ft (192 m.)

305 ft (93 m.)

Pyramid of Giza

455 ft (139 m.)

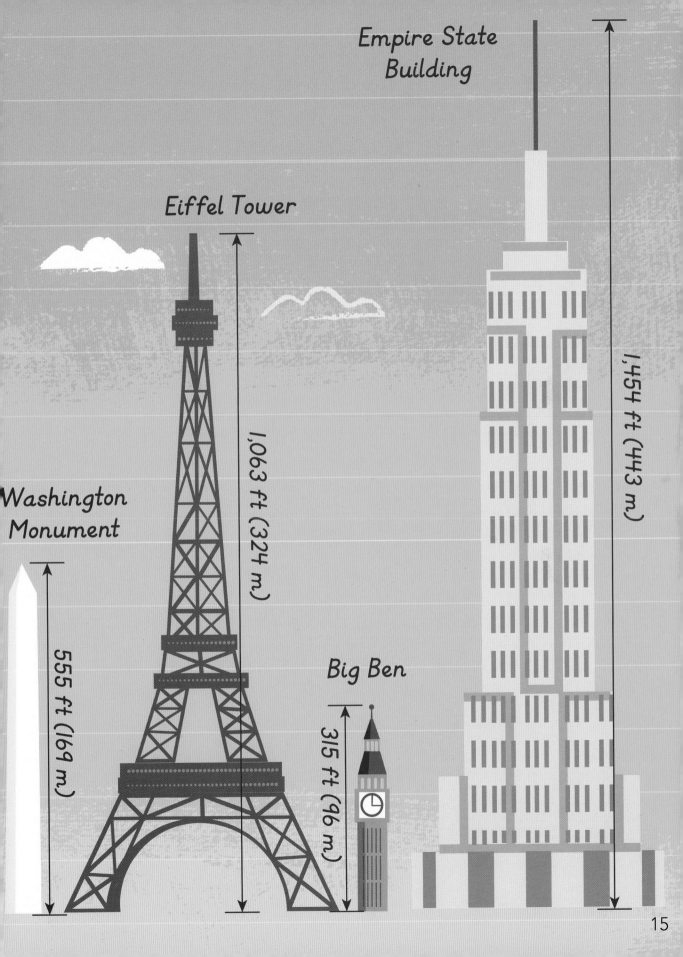

Empire State
Building

Eiffel Tower

Washington
Monument

Big Ben

555 ft (169 m)

1,063 ft (324 m)

315 ft (96 m)

1,454 ft (443 m)

15

Vancouver, BC, Canada

3,437 mi (5,531 km)

Seoul, South Korea 7,714 mi (12,414 km)

With the English System great distances are measured in miles. The distance between Dallas, Texas, and Boston, Massachusetts, is 1,753 miles. Great distances in the Metric System are measured in kilometers. The distance between Dallas, Texas, and Boston, Massachusetts, is 2,821 kilometers.

It's easy to convert miles to kilometers and kilometers to miles.

1 mile = 1.609 kilometers
1 kilometer = .621 miles

Boston, MA

New York City, NY

Chicago, IL

1,341 mi (2,158 km)

1,297 mi (2,087 km)

1,753 mi (2,821 km)

Atlanta, GA

664 mi (1,069 km)

Orlando, FL

228 mi (367 km)

Dallas, TX

Miami, FL

Weight

You are surely familiar with some English System units of weight: **ounces (oz), pounds (lb),** and **tons (tn).** There are other less often used measures including **drams, grains, troy ounces,** and **long tons.**

1 ounce = 28.35 grams   1 pound = 454 grams

In the Metric System weights are all based on the **gram**.

The most commonly used Metric weights are the **gram (g)**; the **kilogram (kg)**, which is 1,000 grams; and the **metric ton (t)**, which is 1,000 kilograms.

Polar Bear

weighs about half a metric ton

Blue Whale

weighs about 180 metric tons

African Elephant

weighs about 8 metric tons

2.20 pounds = 1 kilogram (1,000 grams)

How do English System units of weight compare with Metric System units? Go to your pantry. Look at the labels on a can of vegetables, a box of cereal, and a bag of pretzels. They often have both English System weights and Metric weights on the label.

TUNA
5 OZ (142 g)

Peanut Butter

NET WT
16 OZ (454 g)

Pasta

NET WT 16 OZ
(454 g)

There are 14 ounces or about 400 grams of sugar in this box.

CANE SUGAR

NET WT
14 OZ (397 g)

OATMEAL

NET WT
18 OZ (510 g)

14 oz

Make a list of the English and corresponding Metric measurements. Perhaps you could even make a collection of the labels when the cans, boxes, and bags are empty. If you do, soon you'll be comfortable with both systems of measuring weight.

Pretzels

NET WT 16 OZ (454 g)

Nuts

NET WT 52 OZ (1.47 kg)

POPCORN

ET WT 32 OZ (907 g)

BRAN CEREAL

T WT 12 OZ (340 g)

There are 14.5 ounces or 411 grams of corn in this can.

CORN

NET WT 14.5 OZ (411 g)

411 g

Liquid Measures, Volume

1 quart _

3 cups _

2 cups _

250 —
200 —
100 —
50 —

milliliters

1 cup —
¾ —
½ —
¼ —

1 cup _

Liquids—water, milk, gasoline, and more—are measured by the space they take up, their **volume**. In the United States we measure volume in **cups (c)**, **quarts (qt)**, and **gallons (gal)**. In the Metric System volume is measured in **liters (L)**.

Most containers of milk give the measure of its contents in both English System quarts and Metric System liters. If it's a full quart, you'll see after the 1-quart measure that the milk is .946 liters. If it's a full liter, you'll see after the 1-liter measure that it's 1.057 quarts.

How much is a liter?

A liter is the amount of liquid needed to fill a cube that's 10 centimeters high, 10 centimeters wide, and 10 centimeters deep.

The volume of that cube is 1,000 cubic centimeters.

1,000 cubic centimeters = 1 liter

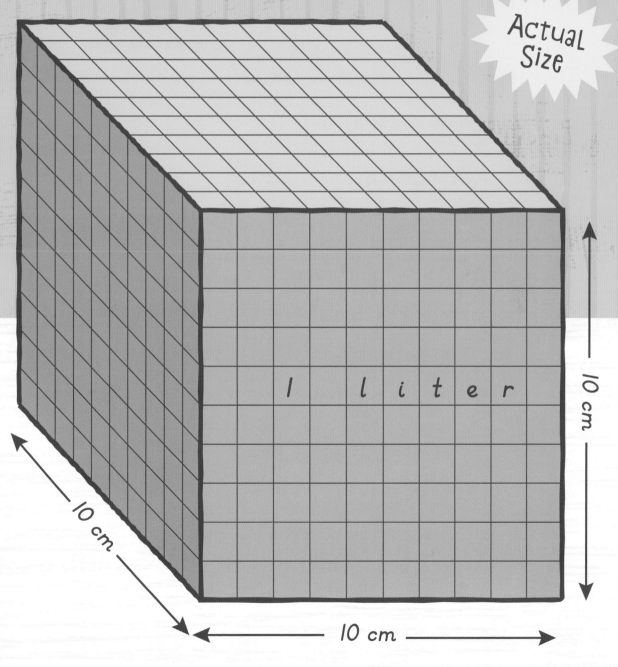

Actual Size

1 liter

10 cm

10 cm

10 cm

10 cm

You can make your own liter cube. Using your inches and centimeter ruler, draw six squares on heavy stock paper or cardboard. Each must be 10 centimeters by 10 centimeters. With safety scissors and adult supervision cut out the six squares. Tape them together to form a cube.

10 cm

milliliters
250
200
100
50

Of course, a liter container does not have to be a perfect cube. The shape can be different, but the volume must be 1,000 cubic centimeters.

There are other measures of volume in the Metric System. They are all based on the liter.

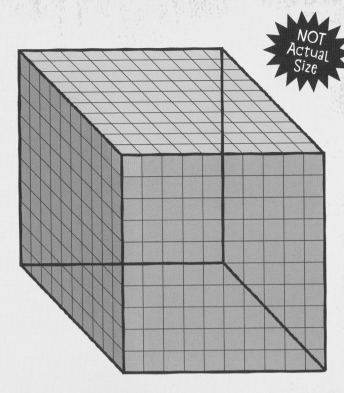

1 milliliter is 1/1,000 of a liter. It's the volume of 1 cubic centimeter.

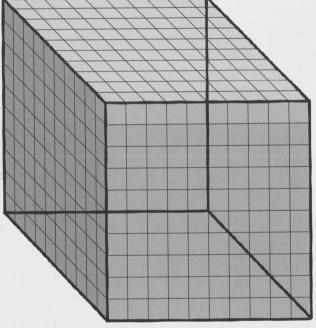

1 centiliter is 1/100 of a liter. It's the same as 10 milliliters.

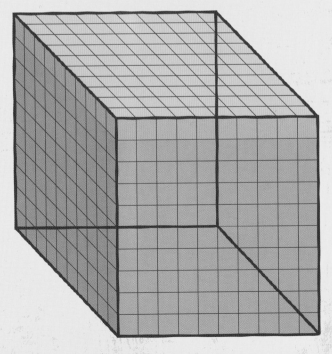

1 deciliter is 1/10 of a liter. It's the same as 10 centiliters and 100 milliliters.

25

1 liter

NOT Actual Size

Remember the power of 10!

1 dekaliter is 10 liters.

1	2	3	4	5
6	7	8	9	10

$$\begin{array}{r} 1 \\ \times\ 10 \\ \hline = 10 \end{array}$$

1 hectoliter

is 10 dekaliters or 100 liters.

1	2	3	4	5
6	7	8	9	10
1	2	3	4	5
6	7	8	9	10

$$
\begin{array}{r}
10 \\
\times\,10 \\
\hline
=100
\end{array}
$$

1 kiloliter is 10 hectoliters

or 100 dekaliters or 1,000 liters.

$$
\begin{array}{r}
100 \\
\times\,10 \\
\hline
=1,000
\end{array}
$$

How do English System units of volume compare with Metric System units? Find a container of some liquid. Look at the label. Most often both English and Metric measurements are listed.

Make a list of the English and corresponding Metric measurements. When the containers are empty, perhaps you could even make a collection of the labels. If you do, soon you'll be comfortable with both systems of measuring volume.

Linear Measures, Length and Distance

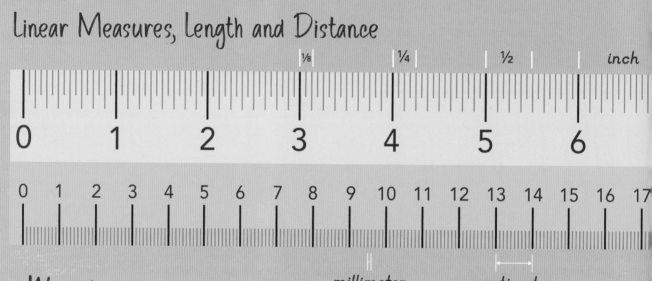

Weight

		Metric	English
•	jellybean	1 gram	.035 ounce
	slice of bread	28 grams	1 ounce
	football	454 grams	1 pound
	7 apples	1 kilogram	2.20 pounds

Liquid Measures, Volume

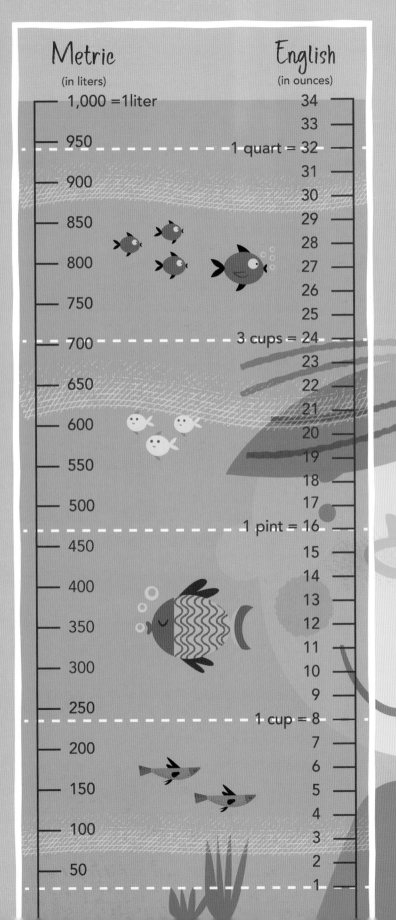

Metric
(in liters)

English
(in ounces)

Metric	English
1,000 = 1 liter	34
	33
950	1 quart = 32
	31
900	30
	29
850	28
800	27
	26
750	25
700	3 cups = 24
	23
650	22
	21
600	20
	19
550	18
500	17
	1 pint = 16
450	15
	14
400	13
350	12
	11
300	10
	9
250	1 cup = 8
	7
200	6
	5
150	4
100	3
	2
50	1

LENGTH

English
1 foot (ft) = 12 inches (in)
1 yard (yd) = 3 feet (ft)
1 mile (mi) = 5,280 feet (ft)

Metric
1 meter (m) = 1,000 millimeters (mm) = 100 centimeters (cm)
1,000 meters (m) = 1 kilometer (km)

English–Metric / Metric–English Conversion
1 inch (in) = 2.54 centimeters (cm)
1 foot (ft) = 0.30 meters (m)
1 yard (yd) = 0.91 meters (m)
1 mile (mi) = 1.6 kilometers (km)
1 meter (m) = 3.28 feet (ft)
1 kilometer (km) = 0.62 miles (mi)

VOLUME

English
1 cup (c) = 8 fluid ounces (fl oz)
1 pint (pt) = 2 cups = 16 fluid ounces (fl oz)
1 quart (qt) = 2 pints (pt)
1 gallon (gal) = 4 quarts (qt)

Metric
1 liter (L) = 1,000 milliliters (ml)

English–Metric / Metric–English Conversion
1 fluid ounce (fl oz) = 29.6 milliliters (ml)
1 quart (qt) = 0.95 liters (L)
1 liter (L) = 33.8 fluid ounces (fl oz) = 1.06 quarts (qt)
1 gallon (gal) = 3.79 liters (L)

WEIGHT

English
1 pound (lb) = 16 ounces (oz)
1 (short) ton (tn) = 2,000 pounds (lb)

Metric
1 milligram (mg) = 0.001 grams (g)
1 gram (g) = 0.001 kilograms (kg)
1 kilogram (kg) = 1,000 grams (g)
1 metric ton (t) = 1,000 kilograms (kg)

English–Metric / Metric–English Conversion
1 gram (g) = 0.035 ounces (oz)
1 ounce (oz) = 28.35 grams (g)
1 pound (lb) = 0.45 kilograms (kg)
1 kilogram (kg) = 35.27 ounces (oz) = 2.2 pounds (lb)

THINK METRIC!

To be truly comfortable with the Metric System you don't want to continually convert inches to centimeters, pounds to kilograms, and quarts to liters. You want to "*Think Metric.*"

Use the Metric side of the ruler you made and measure the width of your notebook, the length of a pencil, the height and width of a box of crackers.

• *Think Metric!*
Make a meter stick. Find a long straight stick, perhaps an old broomstick or a plant stake. From one end, using your Metric ruler, measure and mark exactly 100 centimeters. That's 1 meter. Use your meter stick to measure the length of your bed, your room, the height of your door.

• *Think Metric!*
Go to a supermarket. Find packages with the weight measured in grams—packages of crackers, beans, and cereal. Pick up each of them. What does 100 grams feel like? 225 grams? 500 grams? Find a bag of potatoes or onions with its weight measured in kilograms. Lift them. What does 1 kilogram feel like? 2 kilograms?

• *Think Metric!*
Find an empty water or sports-drink container. Look at the label. Does it measure its contents in milliliters (ml)? In liters (L)? Does it hold 250 milliliters? 500? Does it hold 1 liter? Fill the container with water. Then pour the water into a large empty bowl. What does 250 milliliters look like? 500 milliliters (half a liter)? 1 liter?

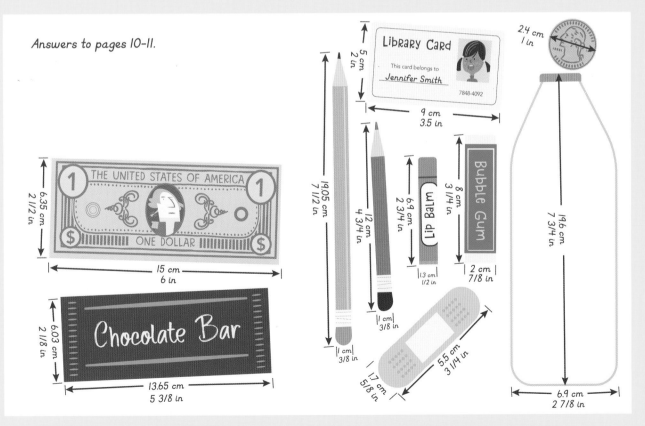

Answers to pages 10–11.

For Mayan Malca, Eyal, Lior, and Sivan —D. A. A.

To my mom —E. M.

Library of Congress Cataloging-in-Publication Data

Names: Adler, David A., author. | Miller, Edward, 1964- illustrator.
Title: The metric system / by David A. Adler ; illustrated by Edward Miller.
Description: First edition. | New York : Holiday House, 2020. | Audience:
Ages 7-10. | Audience: Grades 4–6. | Summary: "An exploration of the
metric system, including centimeters, grams, and liters"—Provided by publisher.
Identifiers: LCCN 2019022773 | ISBN 9780823440962 (hardcover)
Subjects: LCSH: Metric system—Juvenile literature. | Physical
measurements—Juvenile literature. | Weights and measures—Juvenile
literature. | Units of measurement—Juvenile literature. | AMS:
Mathematics education—Arithmetic, number theory—Measures and
units. | Mathematics education—Arithmetic, number theory—Real life
mathematics, practical arithmetic.
Classification: LCC QC92.5 .A335 2020 | DDC 530.8/12—dc23
LC record available at https://lccn.loc.gov/2019022773

Visit www.davidaadler.com for more information on the author, for a list of his books, and to download teacher's guides and educational materials. You can also learn more about the writing process, take fun quizzes, and read selected pages from David A. Adler's books.

METERS	YARDS	INCHES
1	1.093	39.37
.914	1	36

CENTIMETERS	INCHES	FEET
1	.394	.033
2.54	1	.083
30.48	12	1

KILOMETERS	MILES
1	.621
1.609	1

GRAMS	OUNCES	POUNDS
1	.035	.002
28.35	1	.062
453.59	16	1
1,000	35.274	2.205

LITERS	PINTS	QUARTS	GALLONS
1	2.113	1.057	.264
.473	1	½	⅛
.946	2	1	¼
3.785	8	4	1